# THE WHITE RIM TRAIL

## MILE BY MILE

## ROBB MAGLEY

PEREGRINATE PRESS, COLO.

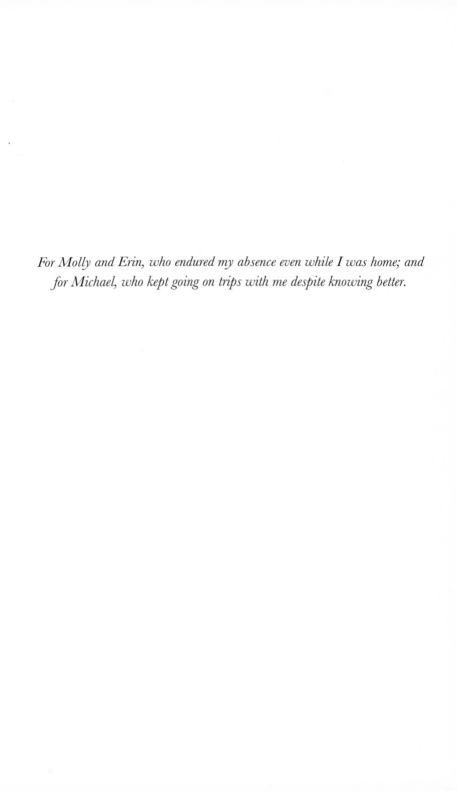

*For Molly and Erin, who endured my absence even while I was home; and for Michael, who kept going on trips with me despite knowing better.*

# CONTENTS

# PREFACE: THE WHITE RIM

There's a great line in the Wilderness Act of 1964, signed into law nine days before Canyonlands National Park was established. The act held that wilderness, strictly defined, must have "…outstanding opportunities for solitude or a primitive and unconfined type of recreation."

Despite some early consideration, Canyonlands of course never became a wilderness area. And as one of the most visited National Parks in the country, it might seem counterintuitive to imagine there are opportunities for solitude here, much less outstanding ones. But outside of the park traffic, off the beaten path, and beyond the pavement, there are few places in this country that are at once so well-loved, and yet feel so empty.

The silence can grab you by both shoulders in Canyonlands. When the wind stops, every footstep seems to make a racket, and you feel almost guilty about coughing, like during the quiet part of a movie. Yet the whine of a passing Jeep engine will be swallowed whole by the still air, long before it's completely out of sight.

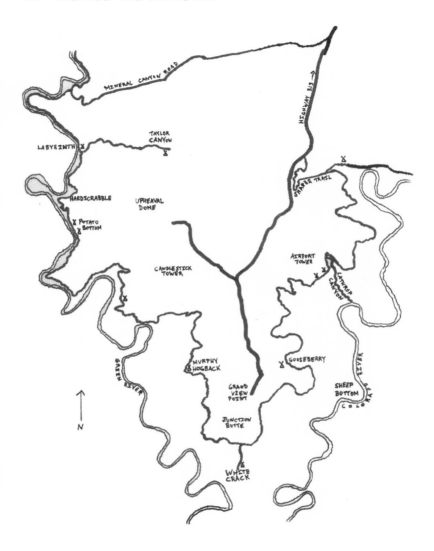

Backcountry permits here are well-regulated, and limited; despite the growth of "overlanding" and the explosion of the Moab area for mountain bikers and Jeep enthusiasts, at the end of the day there are only 20 designated campsites along the entire White Rim Trail, spread out over a hundred miles of dirt road and thousands of acres of steep cliffs and winding canyons.

The names of places and landmarks here range from the fittingly descriptive to the honorific — many canyons, roads and trails are named for the families who eked out a living nearby. There's a story hiding in every sheer wall, in every sandstone slot, and every crumbling hillside; many of them are even true.

*Monster Rock and Washerwoman Arch, from about Mile 18 of the White Rim Trail*

I'm firmly of the opinion that the The White Rim is, by any measure, "outstanding." I hope this book helps you enjoy your time here.

*— Robb Magley*

# QUICK INDEX TO CAMPSITES

# 1

## ON MAPS, MEASUREMENTS, AND OTHER FACTS

Included in this book are a fistful of hand-scrawled maps, meant to deliver the most basic of information without being particularly accurate — by which I mean you'd be a fool not to pick up a properly current map of your own before setting out.

I have also become a huge proponent of GPS and mapping software. Google's satellite maps will give you a great idea of where things are *before* your trip, and phone apps like GaiaGPS show you where you are *during* your trip (spoiler: there's no cell service, much less data, on the White Rim). To that end I've occasionally included geographic coordinates in decimal degrees when it's seemed helpful.

Mileage measurements in this book run "clockwise" — as if driving from Shafer Trail to Mineral Canyon — and will require a little math if you deviate down Lathrop Canyon or the White Crack spur. And they might be less than precise if you make enough turns in one campsite or another to roll your odometer.

Finally, presenting the lore of an area to a reader (you) means someone (me) collecting and curating facts, and that someone (me) can get things wrong. If something's not right, I apologize; let me know and we (you *and* me) can get it sorted for the book's next edition: robb.magley@gmail.com.

*Typical road surface on the White Rim Trail*

## Who can do the White Rim Trail?

I'M GOING to put my foot down here and say "anyone." And then I'm going to qualify that. A lot.

People travel the White Rim Trail in many, many different ways. They do it in four-wheel-drive vehicles, motorcycles, bicycles, even (rarely) on foot and (even more rarely) on horseback. They do it solo, or with friends and family. They do it carrying everything they need to survive with them, or guide-supported with food and water distributed along the way; they do it in their everyday vehicles, or they rent something extraordinarily capable when they get here.

They do it in a single day (mostly on two wheels) or take several. They do it "clockwise" (starting down Shafer Trail and ending at Mineral Bottom Road) or counter-clockwise. They do the whole 100 mile loop, or they go down to a particular spot and come back.

How you do it depends upon how you like to travel, how long you have, and whether you can carry everything you need for the time you plan to spend.

This last part is not trivial; from the moment you leave the pavement until you return, there is no food, no fuel, and no water other than what you bring along. You may see the Colorado or Green River below you, but it is mostly unreachable for miles at a time. And, even when you can access the river, it's a silty brown mess — "too thick to drink, too thin to plow", the old-timers say — that would require hours of settling time before you even begin to treat (or filter) that water. Springs are few, tiny, difficult to locate, and unreliable (and in some places, outright radioactive). So-called "potholes" that sometimes trap water in the sandstone are delicate ecological biosystems that teem with tiny life; on the rare occasion you're lucky enough to find one with water in it, even touching the surface can prove fatal for the living creatures inside. They're also generally small enough that a few sips would be enough to run afoul of the "a water source may not be emptied or depleted for human use" park regulation.

(Plus, let's be honest, it's pretty gross water. Even if you were allowed to, you wouldn't want to. And it wouldn't be enough.)

Hikers and bicyclists — and even motorcyclists, to a lesser degree — find the need to carry enough water to be the most limiting factor. The *minimum* needed (one gallon per person, per day) adds up quickly. The very fit and ambitious on two wheels jam through 100 miles in a single day, and (sort of) solve that problem; mere mortals with a little more to spend can join a supported tour group, where a truck will provide food, water, and even camping gear at every campsite so they can focus on what is one of the most beautiful rides in the world.

Far and away the most popular choice is a personal four-wheel-drive vehicle. My recommendations and observations will mostly center around this sort of travel, but should be helpful for anyone — a mile is a mile, no matter how you cover it.

## What kind of vehicle do you need?

THERE ARE as many opinions on this as there are visitors to the park. The road itself varies, and generally becomes more "interesting" the further away you get from the two relatively smooth entrances to the White Rim — Shafer Trail on one side, and Mineral Bottom Road on the other. Both of these early stretches could be navigated in just about anything that isn't too long for the switchbacks if the weather is dry.

After those first few miles, however, things change. Again, depending on moisture, a stretch of dirt road that is merely bumpy one day can become a mud pit after a good rain. In the best of circumstances, after a long dry spell, drivers face steep, uneven, and slippery graveled terrain in some sections. You'll hear stories of people breaking the rules and going in car like a Prius, and with a bit of luck and a lot of gumption, you might think you could do it too.

But weather in this part of the world is predictable only in its unpredictability. There are trends from year to year, but a forecast becomes useless 36 hours out. Rain can turn a sandy wash into two feet of flowing river in moments; adding water to the fine silt that covers nearly every inch of roadway turns it to a slick wet clay that coats wheel wells and lets tires spin freely.

*The Island in the Sky, from the White Rim Trail*

The penalty for being unprepared is high, and the monetary cost for a vehicle rescue from the local tow companies can top out at two or three thousand dollars.

Four-wheel drive (not all-wheel drive, there is a difference) and high clearance under your vehicle is now *required* by the park service on the White Rim Trail — and plus, it's just sensible. Proper suspension and enough clearance will make the trip more comfortable, you'll have better confidence in the tight and steep places, and you'll worry less about whether you're going to make it and enjoy the country you pass through more.

Don't be tempted to bring an ATV, UTV, or OHV, however; they are not allowed on the White Rim Trail. All motorized

vehicles must be equipped and licensed for interstate travel —
and that includes motorcycles.

---

## How difficult is the road?

THE WHITE RIM Trail is generally described as technically
moderate, with a couple of more difficult sections. Weather can
turn nearly any dirt road into a four-wheel-drive adventure, of
course, but the above description pretty much covers it.

There is not much in the way of technical "rock crawling"
along this road. Stock four-wheel-drive vehicles complete it all
the time. Lifts, winches, and oversized tires will almost certainly
not be needed. Locking differentials are nice but not necessary.
Indeed, apart from weather-related difficulties, the slickrock,
sand, and gravel are easy enough for most trucks to negotiate,
and even the steepest sections won't tax a well-maintained
engine of any size.

It's really more about the driver. Not skill and experience,
necessarily — although those are good things — as much as
being able to keep a cool head in the face of unfamiliar terrain.

The word bandied about here most often is "exposure." As
in, "the road isn't technically difficult, but there's a lot of exposure." This is a polite way of saying "there's a rock wall three
inches from your right mirror, and a 2,000-foot cliff three inches
from your left tires." 99% of the White Rim Trail isn't like this,
of course, but it's only fair to mention that there are places this
describes *precisely*.

In one or two spots along this road, plan on staring down
into the abyss on one side or the other. In a few places, you'll be
climbing so steeply you sort of have to take it on faith that the
road is still down there, out of sight hidden by your vehicle's

hood. Once or twice the turn will be too tight, and you'll probably have to back up a little and take a second swipe at it to get
pointed the right way.

*What* you are driving isn't going to help as much as *how* you
are driving. Stay calm, keep a steady speed, drive the road, and
remember a bunch of people even more frightened than you
made it through earlier. Try to enjoy yourself, laugh long and
hard when you're past the tough bit, and remember there's a
great campsite waiting for you.

## Where do I camp? And when should I go?

BACKCOUNTRY CAMPING in Canyonlands National Park is of
necessity a strictly regulated affair, and the White Rim Trail is
no exception.

All trips, both day trips and overnight, require a permit; on
the backs of those permits are printed a number of regulations
which every visitor is responsible for following. Before you even
*apply* for a permit, however, there are a few things you should
know.

There is no "at large" (i.e. "wherever you like") camping
allowed near the White Rim Trail within Canyonlands National
Park. Unless you're willing to hike at least one full mile from the
road and set-up in a "low-impact area" on the slickrock (and
abide by a host of other backcountry regulations, including
managing your own toilet system), you may *only* camp at one of
the 20 designated sites in 10 designated areas, and they are all
available *exclusively* by reservation. I mean yes, theoretically you
could show up one lovely April morning, and be assigned an
unreserved site for the night. This is not likely.

There is no electricity and no water at any of the sites.

There are no trash receptacles, either — be prepared to take out your own trash.

*Campsite Boundary Marker*

Perhaps counterintuitively, there are quite lovely waterless latrines at each camping area, usually (but not always) stocked with toilet paper. Each site allows up to 15 people and 3 vehicles — each motorcycle counts as a single vehicle, as does each trailer. Every site has a clearly marked boundary, always with corner posts but usually also with a line of watermelon-sized rocks; all your camp activities need to stay inside that boundary.

Pets are prohibited in the backcountry (even if "they stay in the vehicle"), as is hunting, feeding wildlife, and discharging firearms. Campfires also aren't allowed at any of the campsites. With a fire pan, and a willingness to remove every speck of charcoal residue, some outfitters and well-prepared visitors cook with charcoal, but gas and propane cooking is the norm.

RESERVATIONS ARE MADE online at canypermits.nps.gov and can be made starting four months in advance — e.g. April 1st becomes available December 1st. Make your reservations as soon as possible, particularly for multiple-night trips and if you want to pick where you stay; the White Rim Trail is not getting any less popular. The fee as of this writing is $30 per outing, whether you stay one night or a full week in the backcountry. This is however in addition to the National Park entrance fee, which you must pay when you enter; at the time of this writing that fee was $30 per vehicle — $25 for a motorcycle.

When to go? Unsurprisingly, the times of the year when it's tougher to get a campsite reservation naturally coincide with when it's really the most pleasant to be here. Typically these are the park's "temperate" months: April, May, September, and October. High temperatures then tend to be in the 60s and 70s, and the lows fall in the 30s and 40s.

In winter, there can be enough snow for the park service to close sections of the road for safety reasons. And in the summer months, it can get incredibly hot during the day — well over 100 degrees — and you have the added risk of afternoon thunderstorms. Depending upon your trip plans — and how far in advance you're planning — you might look at all the empty slots in August and decide to risk the heat. But extreme high temperatures can make side hikes difficult or impossible; you will use 2-

3 times as much water, and put a bigger strain on your body in general.

This is not to say you can't plan your trip during these other eight "less desirable" months. You will however have to be more prepared for adverse conditions — and it never hurts to just get lucky. I had a wonderful, completely dry and pleasant trip one time in early March; I also experienced an absurdly hot trip in September, which made hiking after 8 a.m. more of a chore than a vacation.

A WORD about flying drones inside Canyonlands National Park: don't. They've been prohibited within the park since 2014.

# 2

# SHAFER TRAIL TO GOOSENECK OVERLOOK

R eset your vehicle odometer after leaving the Grand View Point Road at the Shafer Trail information sign, where the pavement ends (38.471242, -109.811378).

It's worth saying again: after a good rain, *all* surfaces will have a *little* mud, and *some* surfaces will have a *ton* of mud.

0.5 As YOU come around the corner, you catch your first glimpse of Shafer Canyon.

1.0 THE ROAD starts to get slightly bumpy, and you can really see down into the canyon.

1.1 PULLOUTS BEGIN as the road becomes narrow.

. . .

1.5 BE AWARE as blind corners become the norm, with a cliff to your left.

1.6 GOOD PULLOUT TO let traffic by in either direction, with bonus big views.

2.0 LOOKING LEFT and all the way to the canyon floor, you can see the beginnings of the White Rim Trail — and may quietly wonder how you'll get clear down there in such a short distance.

2.2 YOU CATCH your first glimpse of an answer: Shafer Trail's famous switchbacks.

2.4 JUST A LITTLE bit of sand here, coupled with a seemingly low overhang, but fear not: everyone clears it.

2.6 ANOTHER GREAT pull out as the descent begins in earnest.

## The Shafer Trail

THE BEST-KNOWN STRETCH of the White Rim Trail isn't, strictly speaking, on the White Rim Trail at all.

The Shafer Trail is technically a short section of the Shafer Road, descending 1,400 feet in a little less than two miles and "switching back" in tight 180-degree turns a half-dozen times. It is a high-exposure roadway — no guardrails and dramatic drop-offs — but one with a typically smooth surface that's far less steep than it looks. It's smooth enough that with dry conditions it can be driven with a passenger car, and the view into the valley is spectacular enough that hundreds make the drive every day during peak season.

*The White Rim Trail, seen from the top of the Shafer switchbacks*

Like a lot of famous roadways, this one had its humble beginnings as a footpath, the closest thing to an "easy" route from the rim to the canyons below. It gets its name from the Shafer brothers, Frank and John (who went by "Sog"), who ran cattle up and down it at the turn of the century. It might have remained "one cow wide" forever, but the uranium boom prompted a fistful of local entrepreneurs to set bulldozers and dynamite to the task of making it good enough to bring out ore.

The Shafer Trail Road Project self-organized in the summer of 1952, fueled by cash from local businesses, and by Christmas the road was passable. Sadly the nearest "interesting" formation, whose excitation of geiger counters had created perhaps the greatest impetus for construction, turned out to be a dud, uranium-wise. Nevertheless, the Shafer Trail stretch opened up the area below the rim and led to dozens of more substantial discoveries. One or two petroleum companies also sank test wells nearby, although they didn't strike it big.

By 1953, while the uranium boom was in full swing, a huge effort was made over the winter to cut the grade of the Shafer trail down to something more reasonable for larger trucks, or even the "family car" — from a 17% "Jeeps only" road to a "gentle" 14% grade. U.S. Bureau of Public Roads Engineer Roy Jones and Utah State Highway Commission Engineer Alden Newell took credit for the improvement with the local newspaper, noting the importance of the road to the Atomic Energy Commission and the uranium mining interests. But in 1955 maintenance of the road was dropped into San Juan County's collective lap — although some state funds were made available. As the uranium boom fizzled, so did interest in (and funding for) keeping a smooth road down to the White Rim, and the route "roughed up" for several years.

Everyone from the local Rotarians to Jeep enthusiasts from as far away as California had "discovered" the area by the early 60's, and when Canyonlands National Park was established in 1964, the feds brought their checkbooks and the road was kept up once more.

Of course 1967 marked the first Easter Jeep Safari — a tradition that continues today, and has often included at least one trip down the Shafer Trail.

---

2.7 THE FIRST HALF-SWITCHBACK, on a solid 10° downslope, followed almost immediately by your first true 180° switchback. Though narrow and now steep, the road remains in excellent condition — and the advantage of all these switchbacks so close to one another is that you have plenty of opportunity to see traffic coming the other way.

2.9 ANOTHER STEEP 180° switchback, quite tight and to the right. Longer wheelbase vehicles might have to take a second pass at it.

3.1 THIS TIME a 180° switchback to the left, again a tight turn but with plenty of room on the outside for a wide swing.

3.3A VERY LARGE pull out before a 180° tight, steep switchback to the right.

3.4 ANOTHER SWITCHBACK 180° to the left, this time quite a gentle turn, giving you the sense you're almost down.

3.5 ANOTHER LARGE, safe-feeling pullout on the right with great views down canyon. The worst is definitely behind you (as far as the Shafer Trail is concerned).

3.8 YET ANOTHER nice pull out, coupled with your first time driving strictly on a blasted-out rock surface.

3.9THE LAST SWITCHBACK, really more of a right turn.

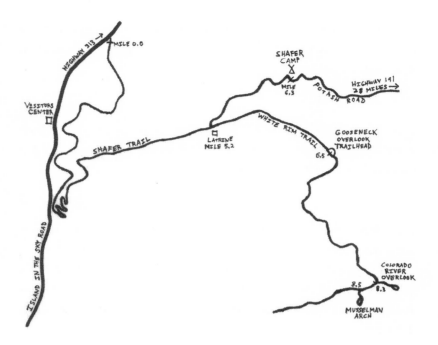

4.0 A few deeper ruts worth paying attention to, but nothing still that cars driven carefully can't navigate.

4.2 FOOTBALL-SIZED ROCKS in the road to help you celebrate being truly down from the Shafer Trail, as well as a nice pull out if you need to catch your breath.

4.4 A LITTLE rocky and rutty, again worth taking slowly in street-oriented vehicles.

4.5 SMALL WASH CROSSING, nothing worrisome when dry.

.   .   .

4.7 ANOTHER NICE pull out on the right, but don't expect to see the Shafer Trail from below — it's all hidden behind rocks from this vantage point.

4.9 ANOTHER SMALL WASH. There is an old abandoned jeep track that carries on for a few miles off to the left, closed to vehicles but if you've got nothing but time, it's not a bad side hike.

5.2 SIGNS (and a latrine) let you know you're at the intersection between the Shafer Trail behind you, the Potash Road to the left, and the White Rim Trail proper straight ahead (38.459400, -109.794708). Moab can be reached after 32 miles via the relatively tame Potash Road, as can the Shafer Camp site after 1.1 miles.

## Shafer Camp

*THE TRIP down the Potash Road to the site of Shafer Camp starts with a narrow, steep, rocky downslope; again, nothing that can't be completed in a carefully-driven passenger vehicle. After the first half mile, some mushroom-shaped pinnacles appear on the right, shortly before a steep drive down in and out of a sandy wash. Shafer Camp is 1.1 miles after the intersection.*

*Busy in the afternoons with folks using the bathroom, Shafer Camp is not particularly flat in the drivable areas, but there's plenty of room for tent campers; no shade but what you bring.*

SHAFER CAMP IS the victim of raised expectations.

In any other park, this would be a spectacular campsite. It's surrounded by canyon walls that do wondrous things during sunrise and sunset; there's a spot (or ten) to pitch your tent with great views down valley, and a latrine just steps from wherever you're camping. There's even a bit of a loop in the driveway here, someone pulling a small trailer could completely avoid backing up with very little planning.

But Shafer Camp suffers because it's just not as good as the other campsites on the White Rim Trail. In fact, technically, Shafer Camp isn't even *on* the White Rim Trail; it's found just past the intersection on the Potash Road on the way to (and from) Moab. This is part of the problem with the site; it is right on a well-traveled road and sees a lot of use. That means the latrine isn't always going to be in great shape, and might be overfull (or out of TP) more often. It also means if you make camp any time before dark — and even after — you'll get a visitor or two on their way somewhere who's going to take a quick stop and use the latrine before they carry on.

Tour groups will stop here, as will multi-vehicle guided tours, and plenty of people who've just hired a Jeep to do the Shafer Trail and Potash Road for the day. And even for those who don't stop, expect to do a lot of waving to people as they go past on their way elsewhere. There isn't, put mildly, great opportunity for solitude here.

Campers who sleep in, on, or attached to their vehicles won't appreciate the small drivable area, either; your choices are close to the latrine (risking odor during unfavorable winds) or close to the road. If parking levelly is a requirement, blocks, rocks, or planks are necessary (tent campers have better spots further from toilet and tours, quite flat and still within the camping boundaries).

So why would you choose Shafer Camp?

The biggest reason it that it's quite near the bottom of Shafer Trail. If you're driving from someplace several hours away and just want to get inside the park before dark, and start your White Rim Trail adventure "properly" the next morning, it's incredibly convenient. After a long highway drive, an evening trip down the Shafer Trail road is beautiful and not too challenging, and from the bottom to Shafer Camp is a mere two miles. It's a decent "utility stop"; kids would likely enjoy exploring the orange rocks behind the site. And again, compared with just about anyplace else, it's got a lot going for it.

You're not going to be miserable here, but you probably won't be exhilarated either.

*The Colorado River from Gooseneck Overlook*

6.5 TRAILHEAD for the Gooseneck Overlook (38.454937, -109.774087). This is a cairned hiking route, rather than an obvious trail through dirt; just head off in the direction you'd suspect and start looking for little stacks of rocks. Follow these to the edge of the canyon, where you're rewarded with a view of the Colorado River and several remarkable balancing boulders.

---

## A Few Words About Biological Soil Crust

YOU DON'T THINK you're going to read this part.

Maybe you already know how important it is to protect Canyonlands' biological soil, and therefore don't think you need to be reminded. Maybe you think you couldn't care less about "some dirt" and want to get on to the neater bits in the book.

But this stuff is almost everywhere out here, it's even more fragile than you think, and it's hugely important.

Looking for all the world like tiny mountain ranges, biological soil crust — sometimes called "cryptobiotic" soil, or if you're old enough you remember it being called "cryptogamic" soil — is made out of bacteria, lichens, and mosses. The bacteria is of a special variety that, like most plants, produces oxygen through photosynthesis; it grows in tiny filaments surrounded by sheaths, and those sheaths are left behind in a complex webbing pattern. The lichens and mosses make their homes in that webbing, and they all work together increasing the soil's stability and its ability to hold in water — which every living thing in the desert needs.

But it's not just retaining the moisture: it's also improving the tiniest topography. In addition to keeping everything from turning into sand dunes, it also turns out these rougher, moister surfaces are *perfect* for seeds dropped by the native plant species. These native seeds have self-burial mechanisms that work great with biological crust; better still, several *non*-native invasive species have trouble with it. Once established, the biological crust creates a nutrient-rich soil underneath it that helps these native plants thrive.

The biological crust is, however, extremely fragile. It can be easily damaged by animals, people, and vehicles. Once the top layer is breached, the entire formation is at risk of collapse; nearby crusts also can be buried by the soil now let loose, and the problem increases exponentially. Regrowing that crust is no easy matter, either; while it generally survives well laying dormant in very arid conditions, it only grows when it's wet — and even then very, very slowly. Many of the "mature" larger crusts you'll see near the White Rim are thousands of years old.

*Biological soil crust, near White Crack Camp*

Under *perfect* conditions, recolonization of the bacteria, lichens, and mosses might take between 50 and 250 years, but those conditions are incredibly rare; what's more, once those soils blow off or wash away, it might be 5,000 or even 10,000 years before that particular spot sees new soil formation to allow it to even *begin* the process.

Back when the only traffic out here was something like one sheep for every thousand acres, the biological crust could keep up. These days it's incredibly important to maintain best practices that help preserve what we have left: keep on existing roads and trails, and walk on the bare slick rock when you have to go cross-country.

# 3

# COLORADO RIVER OVERLOOK TO LATHROP CANYON

E xpect a lovely stretch of road with a cliff on your left as you leave the Gooseneck Overlook, offering beautiful views down into the canyon country.

8.0 SOME RAISED SURFACE HERE, a lot like a speed bump.

8.3 COLORADO RIVER OVERLOOK trailhead (38.438388, -109.766480). Several tire tracks as you head toward the rim prove many people creep their rigs at least part of the way to the overlook, although it's not necessary. It's a shorter walk than to Gooseneck Overlook, with a more expansive view to the river; you can also walk to your right along the rim here towards the Walking Rocks if you want to approach them from here rather than from Musselman Arch.

8.5 MUSSELMAN ARCH pull out (38.437246, -109.770189). The

view of the Walking Rocks from this direction (they're to the left) makes one wonder if they were named because of the seeming possibility of walking over them, or whether it was because several of them seemed to have walked right off the cliff.

*Facing Musselman Arch, west of the Walking Rocks*

## Musselman Arch

Ross Musselman owned the successful 640-acre 4-M Ranch near Monticello. In the late 1940s he and his brother Roy bought out a Moab-area guest ranch in Pack Creek and expanded there; in addition to a successful guide operation that covered the surrounding mountains and canyon country, the Musselman family organized the area's first YMCA summer camp, and secured the concession for horse trips within what was then Arches National Monument.

While Musselman doubtless took some grief from "real" stockmen for his dude ranch, there's no question it was a financial success; when he sold his first ranch out to a Chicago investor in 1950, he pocketed a tidy $30,000 (in 1950 dollars). Musselman spent much of his life promoting the Moab area; from Rotary to the Chamber of Commerce and everything in between, he was about as active in the local community as it could get, and used his rock shop and tour company to take every opportunity he could to introduce people to canyon country. The number of visitors who first saw these orange cliffs under his guidance probably numbered in the thousands. In 1962, as plans for national parks were starting to be set in motion, Musselman hosted the parents of astronaut Scott Carpenter, the first American to orbit the earth.

Musselman Arch used to be known locally as the Walking Bridge, and while I came across a few stories of people who seemed bothered that the man's name was attached to something he didn't discover on his own, it was a lot harder to find anyone who had anything bad to say about Musselman himself. He may not have been the first to see the arch, but he's one of the biggest reasons the rest of us got our chance.

---

8.7 RIGHT after leaving Musselman Arch, a rocky, bumpy stretch serves as a good introduction to what's ahead, and a reminder why high-clearance four-wheel-drive vehicles are required.

8.8 A SMALL ravine that might test your vehicle's approach and departure angles; most won't have any trouble, but I did see evidence of some scrapes.

9.5 To YOUR left is the first finger of Musselman Canyon.

9.7 A SECOND finger of Musselman Canyon, with a nice alcove overhang a short walk from the road. Again there is evidence to suggest some people drive their vehicles to it, but whenever possible, stay on the main road.

10.4 SOME PINNACLE features on the right.

10.5 A FEW larger rocks to take your time driving over.

10.8 "TOOTHY ROCKS" form an interesting backdrop here.

12.3 A SMALL pull out a short walk from the canyon's edge, where you can take in a nice view of the river (38.417950, -109.752395). As always, keep your vehicle within the carefully laid-out line of rocks to avoid damaging the fragile desert on either side of the road.

12.2 SOME ROCK steps to drive down, expect good traction (when dry) and 15° downslopes.

·   ·   ·

12.6 SOME ROGUE vehicle tracks off to the left, where less considerate drivers have gone to inspect some nice balancing rocks. Don't follow them in your vehicle, stop and do the short walk on foot if you must, or drive ahead for a better opportunity in a few hundred feet.

12.8 AN arguably better view of the same balancing rocks.

13.2 TO YOUR left is Little Bridge Canyon.

14.5 SHIFT into 4WD-Low for a short 15° climb up a hill. The backside is slightly steeper (approaching 20°) as you descend, with a rock step or two.

14.8 SOME SMALL ROCK STEPS, worth taking slowly.

15.2 TO YOUR left you can catch your first glimpse of the upcoming Airport Campsites — or at least the latrines for them.

15.8 THIS IS a good view to the left of the upcoming Lathrop Canyon Road, as it descends into Lathrop Canyon toward the Colorado River.

16.0 A TIGHT squeeze past a small rock.

•   •   •

16.3 IN A NARROW side canyon on your left, the white dust of leaching potash is strikingly evident.

16.5 TRAILHEAD for Lathrop Trail (38.401712, -109.794037). There are a few pullouts for parking a little farther down the road on the right.

16.6 THE INTERSECTION with the Lathrop Canyon Road (38.400423, -109.794335), which heads down to the left. It reaches the river's edge in 5 miles, interestingly the only place anywhere in Canyonlands National Park where one can drive to the Colorado River. At the bottom is a lovely picnic area and a latrine, but camping is not allowed there.

## Lathrop Canyon

THE U.S. GRAZING Service first assigned sheepman Howard Lathrop to a winter allotment along the White Rim in the spring of 1939; after a brief exploration of the area, he decided that with a little tweaking he could make it work.

Howard was the sort who saw room for improvement everywhere he looked. In those days, livestock were commonly brought from their summer ranges in Colorado to winter ones in Utah via narrow-gauge train. But if the costs penciled out, Howard would have his men start on foot (and hoof) in October, making the two-month overland journey with his sheep nibbling every step of the way.

When he decided the long, tortuous route down the Shafer Trail was too indirect, he found another one — and made it "sheep accessible" with pickaxe, shovel, and dynamite. Finding the natural potholes in and around the canyon lacking, he built up dams and cisterns with cement, laboriously hauled in via boats and pack mules.

*Monster Rock, from the Lathrop Trail*

As a matter of topography, the Lathrop Road from the White Rim Trail to the Colorado River as it sits today is probably faithful to Howard's original route — there simply aren't a lot of deviations that could be made. But the Lathrop Trail, which meanders up 5 miles from almost the same intersection to the paved road at Island in the Sky, wouldn't appeal in the least to a stockman with several hundred sheep.

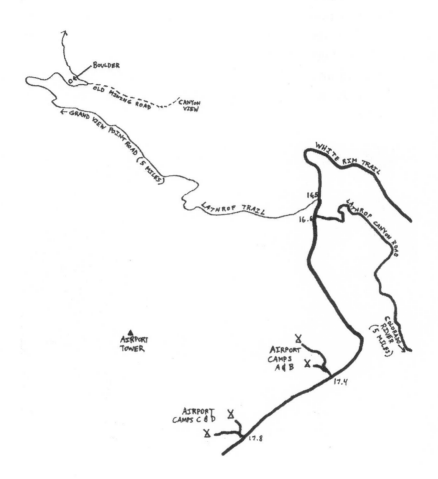

THE FOOT TRAIL deviates from Howard's original route, to the benefit of hikers, and from time to time follows wide, gently-graded roads carved by mining interests. To witness the evidence of one of the more colorful mining chapters in White Rim Trail history, you don't need to hike all 1,600 feet to the top.

The trail follows a river bed at first, leaving it abruptly (keep watching for those cairns around 38.40118, -109.80388) to ascend a footpath until it reaches an old mining track heading northwest. Upon reaching Lathrop Canyon proper, the trail loops back to the east and the attentive hiker will begin to see mine shafts high on both sides. Look down (west) into the canyon from around (38.409112, -109.813033) for a good view into a shaft, as well as one uphill at around (38.408945, -109.813667).

*Signature Rock, Lathrop Canyon*

About 500 feet after the first big switchback (a turn east at around 38.40118, -109.80388) you'll pass a large boulder in the middle of what looks like a great spot for lunch (38.409022, -109.812767). The backside of that boulder is riddled with the carved names of not only stockmen, but also miners — men who started pulling uranium ore out of these rocks at about the same time Howard Lathrop sold off the last of his sheep and began eyeing retirement in Mexico.

---

*If you're comfortable leaving the trail, an old mining road splits off to the east at 38.40892, -109.81132; it's rough and often eroded away, but if you avoid biological soil and scrabbly rocks it eventually leads to a wide shelf and equally expansive view of the White Rim far below.*

---

Collectively, these mines and the mining claims they lie within are known as the "C" Group — not, as I first thought, because all their names started with the letter C (Camel, Cactus, Cesspit, Chump, Crackpot, etc.). In fact, nearly all of the more than 100 claims developed here started with C.

Reading through old claim filings, it seems this "C" group was a sort of pleasant redaction used by the Atomic Energy Commission; in more strictly legal documents, these were known as the Comstock and Crap Groups. Claims within were given names like the Crouch Lode, or the Crop Lode — and, yes, there was a Crap Lode.

In the years following the first filing in 1951, almost 4,500 tons of uranium ore were shipped to a mill from these and other claims within what are now the park boundaries, with twice this amount of rock also removed and left in piles near the tunnel entrances — or used in road construction nearby. For their last several years, the mines produced a fraction of what they had at their peak in 1954, and likely operated at a loss; the owners went to court to convince the government they needed to be reimbursed for their value when Canyonlands National Park was established, but even on appeal were unable to find a judge who agreed there was any profit to be made by 1964.

In 1988 a study was commissioned to determine the best way to protect the public from the radiation dangers posed by particulates in the mine shafts — and in the small, tempting stream flowing through the upper part of the canyon. Ultimately education and warning signs have helped thirsty hikers avoid the contaminated water, and steel rope nets installed in 1990 now block off the shaft entrances — all but ensuring visitors enjoy a radiation-poisoning-free visit to Lathrop Canyon.

# 4

## AIRPORT TO GOOSEBERRY

N otice a little perfectly square flat rock on the right at mile 17.3, like the mortarboard of a graduation cap hanging onto the side of a cliff.

17.4 AIRPORT CAMP sites A (38.392733, -109.795175) and B.

17.8 AIRPORT CAMP sites C and D.

### Airport Camps

*THESE ARE WIDE-OPEN, well-spaced but barren campsites set back from both the road and each other, with the titular Airport Tower as a backdrop; there are plenty of flat places, but no shade but what you bring.*

The four campsites at Airport Camp — Airport A, B, C, and D — are among the more popular along the White Rim

Trail, partly because they represent the first sites that are actually *on* the road, and partly because they are so spacious. These are large, expansive campsites sitting in a large, expansive canyon, with more than enough room for the maximum three vehicles allowed — even if they were carrying a dozen tents each. Bigger groups, such as vehicle-supported bicycle tours, almost always include a stop here.

Airport A and B share an access spur and latrine; B is closer to the main road and latrine, while A is back several hundred yards down a "road" that is just solid slab surface lined with football-sized rocks. Airport C and D have a similar arrangement, a little less than half a mile down the road. In both cases, campers have to decide whether being a little more private is more important than a longer walk to the latrine; I've also heard that if the wind is just right (or wrong) the sites closer to the latrines suffer from odor problems, although I've never experienced this.

Anyone camping on or in their vehicle will have no problem finding a level spot; tent campers should abandon all hope of using tent stakes as nearly every inch of these sites are on solid rock. That said, over the years a good collection of heavy but manageable stones have found their way to these sites as tent anchors, and with good reason: there's often a lot of wind here, inconvenient sometimes but on a hot day a welcome relief.

It's a bit like one imagines camping on the surface of Mars might be: orange, rocky, and solitary. The combination of near-absolute quiet and a view that seems to extend for hundreds of miles can make a solo camper feel particularly alone. That said, voices carry between Airport A and B, thanks to a remarkable echo made possible by the smaller rock cliffs nearby.

All this rock surface is a boon for nighttime tripod-borne photography, of course, as is the wide open sky views afforded here. The Airport Tower itself — the butte that looks like an airport control tower — makes a fine silhouette.

---

17.9 OFF in the distance you can see Washerwoman Arch from an angle that makes it clear it's an arch; as you get closer, the empty space beneath becomes obscured when viewed from the White Rim Trail.

18.9 THE FIRST finger of Buck Canyon is to your left, and you're right on the edge of it. Howard Lathrop would separate his buck sheep from the girls and pen them off in parts of this canyon.

19.3 CLOSE TO a 15° downslope here on good, solid rocks.

19.6 ANOTHER FINGER of Buck Canyon off to your left as you cross a wash. On the far side, as you turn left, is a slightly off-camber stretch of rock road, which is less alarming than it looks. Put your vehicle into 4WD-low and let yourself tilt. No one will come close to rolling here, but there is a good steep hill right after that's a little tight and features a looser surface. A locking differential will make ascents like this effortless at low speeds, but everyone else should simply keep their momentum up and will have no problem.

19.9 THE ROAD is briefly indistinct here, but if you bear slightly to the right you will see dirt tracks revealing the route.

. . .

20.2 A STRETCH of solid rock here is bumpy and rattling; a good test of your loading skills would be to check what came loose on your vehicle after *this* bit.

20.7 THE THREE pinnacles off to the right are features of Washerwoman Arch, now transformed by a completely different perspective.

21.4 AGAIN, Washerwoman Arch is worth looking at from this vantage point, even though the arch itself is hidden.

21.6 A SANDY wash marks the middle fork of Buck Canyon, and a great spot for a picnic.

## Old trees

IF YOU'RE LOOKING for an opportunity to appreciate how small you are, and how brief your tenure on the planet truly is, Canyonlands National Park is a great place to start.

Set aside the massive geological scales involved — the "youngest" rock you will see on the trail is 24 million years old, the "oldest" formed 280 million years ago — and just look at the trees. When I examined aerial photographs from the early 1950s (predating the White Rim Trail's construction), I noticed that the little dots of the trees in the area were in exactly the same spots as they appear on current imagery.

It turns out 70 years is a blip in the lifespan of the two most common trees in the park. A pinyon pine here grows so slowly it might not produce its first cone before reaching 100 years old, and on average lives to be more than 300; the incredible junipers, whose twisted trunks seem to adorn all the best stops along the White Rim, commonly live 700 years — and there are many examples that are more than a *millennium* old.

*Juniper Tree at White Crack Camp*

Put another way, nearly every speck of human history you'll read about in this book took place under the watch of these shade-producing wonders. The same trees. Most of them will still be spitting out nuts and seeds long after your great-great-great-grandchildren retire.

The key to their longevity, of course, comes from an innate ability to set a slow pace. It's good advice for visitors here, too.

---

22.1 SMALL ROCK steps and bumps.

22.2 ANOTHER FINGER of the middle fork of Buck Canyon, and another good picnic spot.

22.3 MODERATE UPHILL SLOPE, but momentum is all that's needed — there's no rocks or other hazards at the top.

23.0 ROUGH AND CRAGGY, choose your line carefully and don't get your vehicle bouncing too much and this should be no problem.

23.6 THE SOUTH fork of Buck Canyon, building its reputation for fantastic picnic spots with flat rocks and gorgeous views.

24.0 A STRETCH of shallow sand, often with a few ruts that indicate how muddy the area can get after a rain.

24.5 A SMALL downslope looks more challenging than it is, you're unlikely to make any mistakes here.

. . .

24.7 THIS DROP into another finger of Buck Canyon's south fork approaches a 15° downslope, made more exciting by the fact it appears you go right off a cliff at the bottom. You don't, obviously; the road turns to the right past some great views. If you're not already, get into 4WD-low for a climb on the other side.

25.8 A 15° downslope here might sneak up on you, but there's nothing to it.

26.3 GET into 4WD-low for this short hill.

26.7 BALANCED ROCKS on your right and standing rocks — much like the Walking Rocks — on your left.

27.2 THE LATRINE you see across the valley marks the Gooseberry Campsites.

27.5 A STEEP-FEELING 15° downslope heads into a narrow squeeze between rocks at the bottom, arriving at the Gooseberry Trailhead (38.335139, -109.828833). Sometimes known locally as the Government Trail — because it was built as a WPA project, and was almost certainly never used by the ranchers it was meant to serve — this narrow, exposed foot trail climbs 1,500 feet in about 5 miles to reach the pavement at the Island in the Sky Road.

. . .

27.6 ONE OF several great spots to stand next to a cliff and have your picture taken from the other side.

28.1 GOOSEBERRY CAMP sites A (on the left) and B. A latrine is on the right.

———————

### Gooseberry Camps

*BETWEEN THE WHITE Rim Trail and a cliff, Gooseberry A has limited shade; uphill Gooseberry B is larger and has the privacy but no shade, plenty of flat in both sites.*

THE TWO GOOSEBERRY camps take their name from the nearby Gooseberry Trail, a 2.7-mile uphill hike that gains almost 1,500 feet before running into the paved road that leads to the Visitor Center at Island in the Sky. The trail was known locally as the Government Trail for years, in no small part because it was originally constructed around 1940 by the federal Work Project Administration; FDR's "New Deal" contributions to the area included improvements like this to make it easier for stockmen to move cattle and sheep. Sometime in the 1960s the park renamed the trail, and fortunately so, as "Government Camp A" just doesn't have the same ring.

You're not particularly likely to find gooseberries at either site, although Gooseberry A has a juniper tree or two, and they cast enough shade to make someone in Gooseberry B a little jealous. But while it looks like they might, the site boundaries at

Gooseberry A don't quite allow you to camp on the edge of the cliff wall. You do get the sense of having your own private abyss nearby, however, at least in the evenings when traffic on the White Rim Trail has died down. A few steps from your sleeping bag will put you perhaps too close for comfort, so situate your camping particulars during daylight hours if at all possible.

Gooseberry B puts you on the same side of the road as the shared latrine, although you're not right on top of it, and it's a larger site with more flat spots as well; the views downhill are as ever spectacular, and you're hugely private with only a short walk to the shared latrine.

As with the Airport campsites, enough wind passes through here to have inspired a lot of football-sized rock collecting, to help keep down corners of tents and tarps. Night skies here are also expansive thanks to a wide valley. With enough time and inclination, Gooseberry Camps' proximity to the trail might be a great reason to stop here — and, of course, the chance to sit on the edge of a cliff with your morning coffee might just seal the deal.

# 5

# SHEEP BOTTOM TO LONESOME CITY

P ut your vehicle into 4WD-low for the rocky uphill stretch
beginning at 29.3 .

29.8 DON'T BE TEMPTED into speed by the smooth road through
here, every now and again there's a big enough bump to knock
you around a bit.

30.5 ON YOUR left is the abandoned dirt track toward the rim
above Sheep Bottom (38.312937, -109.805299). There is room
for two vehicles off the road at a small pull out just before it.

---

## Sheep Bottom

I ALMOST DIDN'T INCLUDE this hike. I did the trek down to the
mining sites above Sheep Bottom on a hot, windless day, and it

was tricky trail-finding and an awful lot of work — much of it made twice as hard as it otherwise might've been by avoiding stepping on the biological soil crust. Between finding the right way down and up, the hike itself, and time spent investigating old mining relics and enjoying the views, it took up the better part of my day, and I was pretty pooped by the end — despite it being really less than two miles each way.

*Colorado River from above Sheep Bottom*

But the views along this hike are pretty amazing — even in a park where amazing views are everywhere. Remember that technically this is a hike to a wide shelf *above* Sheep Bottom, so while there might be a route down to the river from there, I didn't spot it.

There's a good spot to pull off a single vehicle at (38.31404, -109.80496). Google's satellite view will help you see an old dirt road that runs almost perfectly west-to-east, really forming east and a little south at (38.31292, -109.80159).

Once on the ground, however, you'll notice this road isn't much of a road at all these days. The good news is that the desert is reclaiming the disused Jeep track; the bad news is it's barely any easier to follow it, rather than just hiking your way to the rim "off trail."

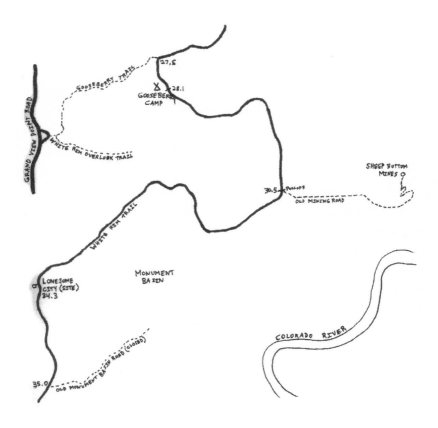

Stepping upon neither biological soil nor plentiful cactus, make your way to an "intersection" of sorts between two abandoned tracks (at around 38.313265, -109.789448), and take the southeasterly trail to another intersection (roughly 38.311265, -109.786067). From here (or from wherever you choose to start) you're heading past several piles of old jars and cans to a quite clear mining road that begins its descent at (38.312095, -109.781508) turning left (northeast).

Where the trail becomes briefly indistinct (around 38.31408, -109.77971), follow it to your left (west) and it enters a tight, often blissfully shady, canyon and continues to descend. Take a look back uphill when you get down from these switchbacks (38.315487, -109.781687) to be sure you can find your way back up, then feel free to explore the mining debris and great viewpoints (the latter are found, of course, above the river to the east). There are a number of mining markers that, if you bother to note them all and plot a map later, form the squares of the old uranium and vanadium claims the road was built to develop. Resist the temptation to remove anything you find and leave those "discoveries" for the next person.

---

31.2 IN THE distance as you look left on a clear day, you can see the points and spires of the Needles District.

31.6 ALL THE white rock on your left is White Rim sandstone, the trail's namesake; the spectacular formations in the canyon below mark Monument Basin, one of the most photographed areas in Canyonlands. In 1965, the U.S. Board of Geographic Names officially stamped its approval on "Monument Basin," an accuracy-laden compromise between "Monument Canyon" (what locals had always called it) and "Standing Rock Basin" (what climbers had started calling it). It is a basin (rather than a canyon) by definition, being neither open on just one end nor longer than it is wide.

·   ·   ·

31.9 A SMALL pull out here makes a great base of operations if you mean to take photos. The light is best here often in the early morning, or late in the afternoon.

*Monument Basin*

32.1 Speaking of photos, if you're traveling with a friend, stop here and let them go ahead; they're about to drive right on the edge of the lip you see across canyon, and this is a good spot from which to capture it on film.

32.3 THIS FUN little stretch is divided by a small bush; go to the right and it's slow, rocky going. Go to the left, and things are smoother, but you're driving right on the edge of the cliff — and more excitingly, the rock beneath you is undercut. Notably it hasn't broken off, yet.

·  ·  ·

32.4 A SLIGHT (10°) upslope here may require 4WD-low.


33.0 ON YOUR LEFT, still, is Monument Basin.


33.1 A 20° downslope here is steep, but smooth and straight.


33.8 ANOTHER 20° downslope here, going slow will keep you in control. Also it drops into yet another great spot to view Monument Basin.


34.3 THE FLAT area on the right here is likely the site of Lonesome City, and the beginning of the hike up the mining roads its inhabitants built.


## Lonesome City

WHEN A FRIEND of the editor at Moab's Times-Independent took a drive down the relatively-new Shafer Trail road in the summer of 1954, he brought back a lighthearted tale any good newspaperman would be a fool not to share:

"Down under Grand View Point, we came onto a sign which read 'Lonesome City, Approximate Elevation 5,000, Population 3.' We were surprised to find a new town, but were unable to meet any of the citizens as they were all out prospecting."

A follow-up story three weeks later (because stuff like this is half the fun of running a newspaper) concluded that Lonesome

City's inhabitants were, in fact, a team of road-builders working to help Midwest Uranium access a handful of claims on the shelf between Junction Butte and Grand View Point. Midwest was in the process of becoming something of a uranium juggernaut; by the mid 1950s, they had absorbed a half dozen other mining corporations in the area to hold nearly 900 claims in Utah, Colorado, Wyoming and South Dakota.

The site of Lonesome City is still a fine place to leave the White Rim Trail for an overland route up to the old mining area; a more detailed description of the walk will be covered in a later edition, but the adventurous hiker can leave the White Rim Trail road at (38.29964, -109.85187) and follow the faint path west for about a mile until reaching a cut mining road near (38.296184, -109.867313) that climbs up (and north) to the area of the old claims. Since the old roads are practically invisible at ground level, scouting a route beforehand via satellite imagery is necessary — or a careful examination from the Grand View Point Overlook might work, too.

As for Lonesome City itself, the last we heard of it was again through the editor of the Times-Independent:

"...Expected to hold an election to decide who was to be mayor, city clerk, and treasurer, with the biggest fight expected for the position of the person who would handle all the sheckles. They did not know whether to cut cards, or draw straws to settle the controversy. Then their wives came onto the scene and took over, settling it at once. The boys seemed quite pleased over the outcome."

# 6

# MONUMENT BASIN TO CANDLESTICK

W atch for a stack of twisted logs on the left at 35.0, marking the closing-off of an old road towards another viewpoint into Monument Basin. As recently as the 90s — the 1990s, that is — this was still open to vehicles. The faint track can still (and should) be hiked, of course, for a less-seen vantage point into this wondrous valley.

35.2 AN even fainter spur here used to head toward the same now-closed road to overlook Monument Basin from the south.

35.9 ON YOUR right is a curious square boulder that gives the impression of having slid halfway down the hill and stopped, all by itself, to be framed against the blue desert sky.

36.1 AN UPSLOPE here is only about 10°, but could seem alarming as it's not clear what lies over the crest. It comes down straight ahead on the other side, only slightly steeper, and arrives at the intersection with the White Crack Road (38.274678, -109.863250). Exactly 1.4 miles down this bumpy, often sandy road lies the White Crack campsite (38.257542, -109.865783).

---

## White Crack Camp

*THIS IS one of my favorite campsites anywhere, featuring absolute solitude by sunset, a short walk to the edge of the White Rim, and some of the best views in the park.*

*View to the southeast from White Crack*

YOU MAY HAVE HEARD a night spent at White Crack Camp is an absolute necessity for any trip. This is completely true.

*The "crack" mining road south of White Crack Camp*

The campsite itself marks the southernmost point you can drive within the Island in the Sky district, lying at the end of a 1.4-mile spur off the main White Rim Trail. It's geographically about midway, although you're technically a few miles closer to the Visitor Center than you are to the top of the Mineral Canyon switchbacks.

Within the camp boundaries are two areas: a lower, more protected area with a nearby grove of shade trees, and a higher, rocky shelf that most vehicles can climb and set up atop. The latter makes for the most spectacular views in nearly every direction, although it can feel a little exposed when the wind picks up, and there's no shade to be had up there.

If you arrive during the afternoon, you will likely have company; a walk out to the tip of the peninsula here is uncommonly rewarding. Between the numerous active "potholes" and a standout view, few tour companies skip at least a short stop here. But by early evening, anyone who doesn't have that reservation for White Crack's single campsite has to be on the move — if they want to get where they're going before dark. That's when the small parking area adjacent to the trailhead empties, and you'll have this magic spot all to yourself.

You can't physically drive farther south than the White Crack Camp, although years ago the gap in the rock to the south was blasted out to make a very rough 4WD track (38.255206, -109.866140).

That "crack" was originally used by ancient people who traveled through this area, and was widened for cattle by none other than the Murphy Brothers Cattle Company (see page 60) around 1918. It was enlarged further by uranium miners in the 1950s — close inspection of the walls will reveal the vertical holes drilled for dynamite.

While at one time a Jeep could make the trip, today the road is closed to vehicles, degraded to where it's only suitable for hiking — and even then it's an ambitious walk down to the mining area it was meant to serve. Details for that hike will be in a later edition, but the adventurous can follow the old road down as far as they feel comfortable hiking back.

---

36.7 PULL OFF with pinnacle views, followed by bouncy rocks.

•   •   •

37.2 ANOTHER NICE pull off with wide-open canyon views.

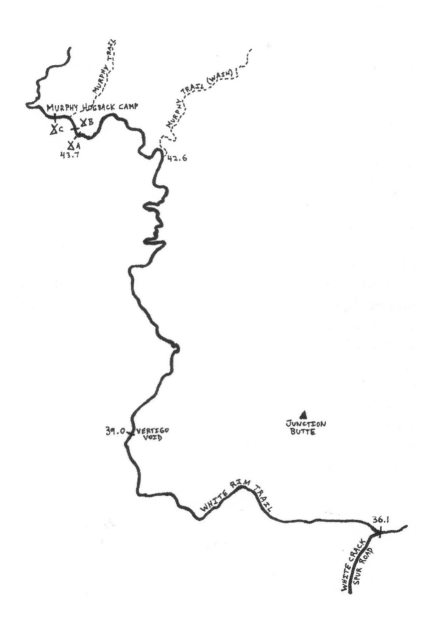

37.4 LOOKING BACK to your left you can see the White Crack in the distance.

37.6 SHORT, not too steep climb that may require 4WD-low.

38.4 BEAUTIFUL WHITE rim sandstone cliffs ahead of you, all slightly undercut and all painted with "desert varnish," a slow-growing dripping lichen that dries black in the sun.

*The road runs quite close to the undercut cliff edge*

39.0 Yet another beautiful cliffside pull-off picnic spot. A popular stop due to the undercut rock you can creep to the edge of; some guides have taken to calling this spot the Vertigo Void, suggesting visitors lay on their stomachs with their chins just over the edge and look down, then out. It's thrilling and unsettling, but frankly doing this *anywhere* along the White Rim would likely have the same dizzying effect.


39.7 THE LONG climb above the White Rim proper begins with a short rock slope that is probably best tackled in 4WD-low.


40.2 YOU CAN SWITCH BACK OUT of 4WD-low here for roughly a mile of easier driving.


41.1 SWITCH back into 4WD-low here, this is the only-slightly-challenging beginning of the climb up to the Murphy Hogback. A hogback is a ridge with a sharp summit and steep, sloping sides; this hogback, the hiking trail, and the nearby wash were all named for the cattlemen who built the original path here around 1911. A 15-20° upslope will seem effortless with a differential locked, but again simply keeping steady speed will win the day.


41.3 IN ALL THE EXCITEMENT — specifically a tight right hand turn here — don't forget to enjoy the views! A particularly nice one emerges on the left. At the top of this upslope is another tight turn, this time to the left.


41.9 GREAT PULL off with a down-valley view on the left.


42.0 A 15° downslope here is straight, and only a little bumpy.

.  .  .

42.2 A SHORT 20° downslope here has good visibility but can be slick after a rain, but otherwise should be no problem.

42.6 CROSS MURPHY Wash here and its titular trailhead, followed by a 20° upslope that gently turns to the left.

---

## Murphy Trail

ALMOST UNBELIEVABLY, given the steepness near the top, this trail was built for cattle and cattlemen on horseback — and used that way, beginning around 1918. Five of the seven Murphys — Tom, Jack, Otho, Will, and Vic — ran cattle up on what would become the Island in the Sky and down beneath Grand View Point, using the then-narrow Shafer Trail to move them higher and lower.

Shafer Trail was, however, not particularly direct for them, so in 1917 they pioneered another route down the side of the mesa and into the wash that would eventually bear their name. The following year they brought the first cattle down their trail, and back up when the grazing on the mesa improved. It was an endeavor that would only last a few years — the Murphys were out of business here by 1920.

The Murphy Trail can be hiked as a 10-mile near-loop (more like a tennis racquet shape) up through Murphy Wash, switchbacking to the top of the mesa, back down and over the Murphy Hogback, finally reconnecting via a short stretch of the White Rim Trail. There's a neat little bridge offering good purchase through one of the steeper sections, originally laid down by J. Adiart and Darwin Allies, who worked for the Murphys' cattle operation. The bridge today has been restored, made of wooden planks instead of round timbers.

---

42.9 ANOTHER STEEP, but relatively short, 20° upslope.

43.0 THIS 15-20° upslope is a bit of a rocky mess, starting slightly off-camber; again, a locking differential will eat this up, but it's not necessary.

*The final climb up Murphy Hogback*

43.3 THIS IS IT! The notorious climb to the top of the Murphy Hogback that stars in everyone's trip videos rises in front of you. 4WD-low is *mandatory*, and your ascent will be easier with differentials locked, but vehicles without lockers accomplish it daily. The first few yards are the most difficult, with larger loose rocks; after that it's a simple (if narrow and exposed) steep climb, with one last big step at the top to make sure you're paying attention.

43.7 THE TOP of the climb. You've arrived at the first of the Murphy campsites.

---

## Murphy Camps

*THESE SPECTACULAR SITES offer camping on top of a mesa, with great views in every direction from sites A and C; site B is more out of the wind. A few trees means a little shade.*

FOR MANY WHITE Rim Trail travelers, the climb up to the Murphy Hogback is the highlight of the trail — and the exciting ascent is deserving of a proportionally special camp. The three Murphy Hogback sites are just that: they're well set apart from each other, considering the small area. Two are practically right on the cliff's edge, and the third is set snugly back.

Murphy A is as "on the cliff" as any campsite is going to get, even staying within the camping boundary markers. With a couple of small trees and a fantastic large mushroom-shaped rock, you've got nice shade possibilities and an interesting topography. View-wise, Murphy A might be better than C, but at best only slightly.

On the other side of the road, Murphy B boasts a juniper tree or two, and a good rock bench for kids (or adults) to play on. It's not a huge site, and vehicle campers might have to spend a little more time finding a good level spot, but they're there. Murphy B is closest to the second Murphy Trailhead, which lies between B and C. Murphy A and B share a latrine, and it's significantly closer to A, presenting a bit of a trudge from B — particularly at night. On the other side of the coin, nearly everyone who tops out the Murphy Hogback road is ready for the latrine; if you stay at A, be prepared to wave and nod as people stop for the facilities.

Sort of feeling like it's on the way out, Murphy C has lots of junipers, a couple of rock benches, and feels the most protected of the three. It also has its own latrine. A very short walk leads to a spectacular view pull out right across the road, sadly just outside of the camping boundaries but close enough to enjoy well into the evening. A short trail from Murphy C to the west leads to a peninsula that rivals White Crack, view-wise, and might be the best sunset spot in the entire park.

---

43.9 THE OTHER Murphy Trail trailhead is here.

44.1 MURPHY CAMPSITE C. From here the descent begins with a straight but rocky downslope, 15-20°. After the ascent, this will seem easy, if narrow.

44.3 A STEEP 20° downslope approach into a right hand turn here gives you the feeling you're almost finished with the Murphy Hogback.

44.5 SOME ROCKY steps going into a right right turn. An overhang here is actually taller than it looks, but for vehicles with a lot of height — camper shells on high trucks, for instance — it's probably worth getting a spotter.

44.7 YOU MIGHT THINK it's safe to get out of 4WD-low for a while here, but there's a steep uphill just ahead worth staying in low gear for.

45.6 A STEEP, sandy, rocky 20° downslope.

46.0 A SHORT hill here will turn to the right at its crest, a blind turn you'll have to trust is there.

46.2 Two NARROW and tight turns here, followed by a slippery 15-20° upslope.

46.4 ANOTHER LOOSE rock and sand 20° downslope.

46.7 THIS UPSLOPE turns to the right as you climb, with a few larger rocks in the mix that are worth paying attention to.

47.0 IF YOU NEED A BREAK, stop here with a beautiful view of Candlestick Tower straight ahead.

47.1 A VERY SANDY 20° downslope here.

. . .

47.2 TAKE a deep breath an feel free to switch out of 4WD-low for a while here, the worst is behind you.

47.7 NICE PICNIC spot with great views of Candlestick Tower and the surrounding white rim sandstone.

47.8 ONE MORE GREAT spot to stop and let your friends go ahead for a picture; they'll be driving next to the boulders you see next to the cliff just up the road.

47.9 YOUR FRIENDS should park here for their picture, but with a reminder not to get too close to the edge — it's *significantly* undercut.

48.1 SMOOTH SANDY STRETCH, keep your momentum.

48.4 A ROCKY, sandy, and loose 15° downslope lands in a soft bit of sand here.

48.5 DEPENDING on the light conditions, this is another spot to let your friends go ahead for a snapshot.

48.6 BE in 4WD-low for a short scrabbly section here, keeping up your momentum is helpful.

. . .

48.7 YOUR FRIENDS should park here for their picture.

49.0 A 15° downslope here shouldn't be challenging this far into your White Rim Trail experience.

49.3 SWITCH into 4WD-low here to manage a short hill; a lot of loose rock here, it's worth having the traction.

49.4 ANOTHER SANDY stretch that requires keeping yourself on the move.

49.8 CLIFFSIDE WHITE Rim sandstone picnic spot, with Candlestick Tower dominating the landscape to the right.

50.6 ENJOY a smooth bit of sandy road here. None of this is deep, just comfortable shallow sand.

50.8 ANOTHER PICNIC SPOT, if you need a break. Looking to the left you'll spot some beautiful spires and well-varnished White Rim sandstone.

51.1 OFF to your left (and across the river) is your first view of the Turk's Head tower. It was well-known to Ancestral

Puebloans, but petroglyphs and ruins are all on the other side of the river.

*Turk's Head*

51.7 SEVERAL WIDE places on the road here provide parking if you want to walk to the rim and get a better view of the Turk's Head. More excitingly, if you walk slightly east as you head towards the rim (slightly to the left), you're going to run into the west end of a formation called the Black Crack — a fracture more than 1,700 feet long and just one or two feet wide. And a long way down; watch your step.

51.9 SWITCH into 4WD-low here for a few rock steps.

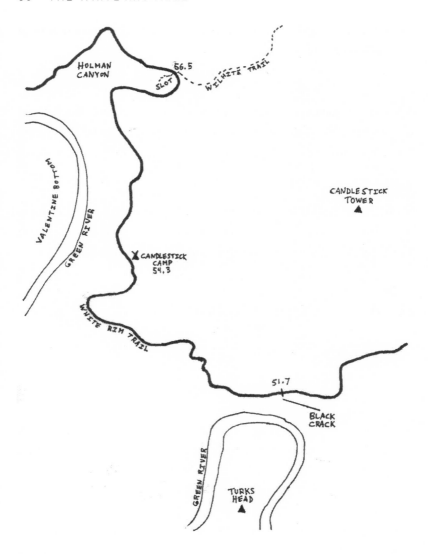

52.2 THE UPSLOPE here is loose rock and turns to the left; switch into 4WD-low if you aren't already in low gear. It's a blind top, but you'll want to stay to the right to immediately go left; if you go straight, there's a big step down where you might scrape your vehicle's underside. Stay in low gear for a while, there's plenty of rough and loose rock ahead.

52.5 A SCRABBLY, sandy, loose and steep (20°) downslope here, but it's straight and there's plenty of opportunity to see to the bottom of things.

53.6 A PISTIL-SHAPED protuberance appears in the distance. This thin tower sits atop Hardscrabble. Just across the valley you'll catch a glimpse of Candlestick Camp's latrine.

54.3 ARRIVE at the site of Candlestick Camp.

## Candlestick Camp

*THE CAMPSITE itself is pretty barren, but it's right across the road from your own personal cliff. Plentiful tent spots make this popular with mountain biking groups; there's no shade here but what you bring.*

ANOTHER WIDE-OPEN CAMPSITE right across the road from a spectacular White Rim sandstone canyon, staying the night at Candlestick Camp is a solitary affair; you won't have to share space with anyone, although that unfortunately includes "trees" because there aren't any.

Interestingly, apart from a sandy pull-through which vehicle campers will find good and level, almost the entire site sits on White Rim sandstone, which makes it a unique camping experience on the White Rim Trail. There's plenty of space here for dozens of tents, and an easy stroll across the road to a cliffside hangout where sunsets are spectacular. Of course the nearby Candlestick Tower dominates the skyline, but don't expect it (or anything else) to cast any shade on your camp.

You won't have to share the latrine, since it's a single-site camp, and it's situated just across the road — far enough away to assuage any odor fears, but close enough to get to after dark. Like several of the White Rim Trail campsites, it's a bit in the middle of the view, however, so the latrine winds up in a lot of photographs at Candlestick Camp.

# 7

# HOLMAN CANYON TO POTATO BOTTOM

E njoy the soft ride on comfortable sand through this stretch leaving Candlestick — while it lasts.

55.5 TO YOUR LEFT, and across the river, is Valentine Bottom. The Valentines made their home there for just over a year before moving back to town, but the name stuck.

55.9 AS YOU turn the corner here, the narrow canyon on your left is Holman Canyon, named for sheepman Emery Holman; looking backwards, you can see Candlestick Tower from a very different angle.

56.2 FROM THIS PERSPECTIVE, I've always thought Candlestick Tower looked a bit like a queen facing to the right, and across the saddle behind her is an attending large-nosed dwarf. On my last time through, I thought the "queen" also looked a bit like George Washington, hat and all.

56.5 USE the small pull off here to explore Holman Slot or the Wilhite Trail.

*Holman Slot*

## Wilhite Trail and Holman Slot

THE WILHITE TRAIL is another route up to the Island in the Sky, this time covering the 1,500 vertical feet in a little less than 6 miles. What's always struck me about this trail is how little we know about its namesake. "Wilhite Trail" was written on the side of a rock adjacent to the trail, probably by someone with that name who at least helped build it. And the name stuck. There have been Wilhites living in Moab for decades, but I've had no luck discovering which among them might've scrawled his way to fame.

Directly across the White Rim Trail from the Wilhite Trail is an easily-missed slot entrance to Holman Canyon. Use caution if you decide to drop into it, and never go alone, because the walls are steep and can be slick. As a rule of thumb, look at everything you climb down and try to imagine how you're going to climb back up later; if it looks questionable, stop there and call it a day.

It's a beautiful narrow slot with a sandy bottom and several picturesque puddles, but really doesn't extend more than a few hundred feet before an impassable 80-foot cliff ends even the most ambitious foot traffic.

---

57.6 NICE PICNIC spot looking across to Valentine Bottom — marked by the large trees you can just barely see.

58.0 THE RIVER comes into view — remember on this side it's now the Green River, not the Colorado.

·  ·  ·

58.8 LOOKING TO YOUR LEFT, the white rim sandstone is thick enough to have made interesting shapes — mini buttes and worn out slopes and peaks — and across on the other side the thickness is accented with desert varnish.

59.9 POINTY ROCKS THROUGH HERE, watch the sides of your tires.

60.0 ANOTHER GLIMPSE of the river.

60.2 WIDE SPOT in the road here is a great parking spot if you'd like to walk out to the rim for the river view.

61.1 ALL THE lush greenery below sits on Queen Anne Bottom, the trail to which is coming up shortly. The mysterious "Anne" made her home down there for a few years before 1920, and briefly operated a flat-bottom boat ferry service before moving on.

61.3 A SMALL turnoff here marks the old road down to Queen Anne Bottom. Closed to vehicles now, of course, but it's a short (if often brambly) walk to the river. At one point a few years after Anne left, a newer livestock ferry on cables crossed to the other side here, and some metal anchoring hardware can still be seen in rocks at the shore. In dryer years, cattlemen could cross with their herd just walking on the gravel that spilled from Millard Canyon on the far side of the river.

· · ·

61.8 ON THIS side of the river, ahead and on the left, is the south edge of Beaver Bottom.

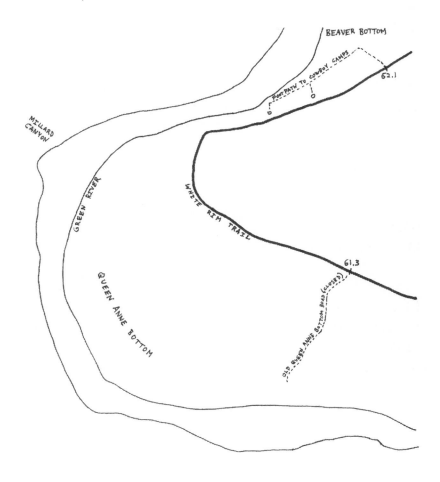

61.9 A SMALL pull off here is almost directly above the Beaver Bottom Cowboy Camp, but you can't get down right here.

62.1 WHEREVER YOU find to park, right here is the best spot to descend (38.394589, -110.020281). There are gentler slopes to the bottom down the road a third of a mile or so, but it means a lot more walking through the ample cactus fields once you're down. Right here isn't too serious a scramble, and puts you much closer to the two sets of inscriptions. A faint footpath near the rock wall heads downriver to the site.

*Green River at Beaver Bottom*

## Beaver Bottom Cowboy Camp

Tucked under an overhang and reached via short scrambles to narrow ledges, the inscriptions at the south end of Beaver Bottom are mostly those of cow hands, dating from 1925 to as late as 1947.

Allred brothers Ephraim and Gilbert worked for Art Murray running cattle in the 20s; Kenneth Allred and Vaughn Taylor worked for Cecil Thompson in the late 30s and early 40s. For all of them, a nice stone shelter like this was the perfect place to wait out a storm — and write your name a few times, it seems — before heading their stock out toward Mineral Canyon and civilization.

Arthur Wheeler, who wrote his name here much earlier in 1891, came to the Green River's edge in 1884 to grow alfalfa and plant a fruit orchard. With his two brothers he also ran a few cattle, but his local claim to fame was as part of a plan to pilot steamboat excursions down to Spanish Bottom. A few trips were made with Wheeler at the helm, but steamboat tourism never quite took off the way he and his partners had hoped.

Wheeler left Utah for the Yukon Gold Rush in 1898, but his inscriptions can be found in a couple of spots in and near the park.

---

63.8 If you look upriver, you'll see a single large tree that marks Potato Bottom A Campsite.

63.9 A nice wide pull off with a great view of the river here.

64.2 An inconveniently placed rock here makes a narrow road even narrower; wide vehicles may want a spotter.

64.3 Right about here you're directly above the Potato Bottom Cowboy Camp, but again you need to go just down the road to find a place to park and walk back.

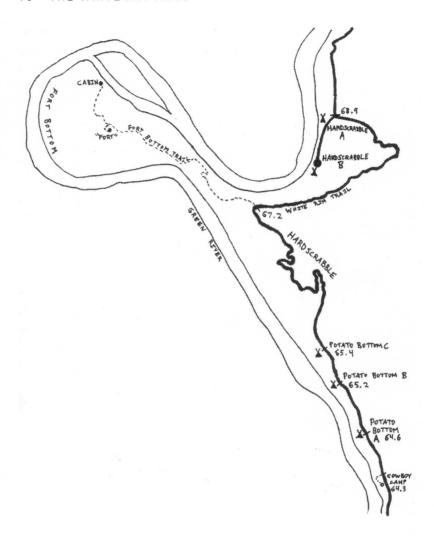

## Potato Bottom Cowboy Camp

Just like back at Beaver Bottom, this is a little alcove under a rock overhang that was used by cattlemen for shelter; Potato Bottom was the last "good" watering hole for cattle and horses before heading up above the Green River.

At this spot, however, no one appears to have left their mark;

the highlight is an old trunk that's approaching 100 years old at this point and is little more than steel bands and latches. Art Murray seems to have hauled it down to keep supplies for the men who worked for him sometime in the 1920s, and it's stayed put ever since.

*Art Murray's trunk at Potato Bottom Cowboy Camp*

This is a neat little place that probably wouldn't be worth a long hike — which fortunately there isn't. Wherever you choose to park, walk to roughly (38.41744, -110.00191) and take a quick route down with a little scramble. Once down off the rock here you're just a few steps downstream (turn left) to the alcove. I'd request visitors to this little alcove not even touch the old trunk at this point, it's just barely keeping its shape. Enjoy the space, take a picture, but leave things be.

It's a bit of work to get back up at the same point, so if it proves too much you can walk along the base of the rock until you see an ascent more to your liking.

64.6 SITE A, Potato Bottom Camp. From the road here, ahead in the distance, you can see a small pinnacle next to the butte a ways ahead — that's up on the Hardscrabble (see Chapter 8).

64.9 A FEW deep ruts here, and yes, it's a mud pit after a rain.

65.2 SITE B, Potato Bottom Camp.

65.4 SITE C, Potato Bottom Camp.

---

## Potato Bottom Camps

*FRIENDLY TREES ADORN these usually sandy, sometimes muddy, and often buggy camps later in the summer. Cliff walls are the views, and while the river is nearby, it's hard to get to. But there's plenty of shade.*

THE CAMPSITES at Potato Bottom get a bit of a bad rap, but the problem is we're just expecting them to be so much better.

These sites are as close to the river as any in the Island in the Sky district, which seems like it might make them desirable. Unfortunately, it's difficult to get down to the river from any of them, thanks to thick brush, and when you get there you discover there usually isn't anything like a beach or sandbar to sit upon to enjoy the water. Moreover, aside from early spring and late fall (and obviously winter), being close to the river means mosquitoes thrive here.

Couple all this with a propensity for these sites to turn into mud pits after a healthy rain and you've got more than a few people who will tell you they absolutely hated Potato Bottom.

But after so many miles of rock and sand, the enormous trees here are practically begging you to stop and rest in the shade beneath them; and when they're dry, all of these sites are spacious and level. The views aren't expansive, of course, but the cliff walls to the east light up a beautiful fiery rose color at sunset.

Potato Bottom A has a giant tree that casts enough shade to cover more than one vehicle, and boasts its own latrine. It is however close to the road, and more than a few folks will stop to use it during the day. Potato Bottom B is a nice sandy site with a couple of trees that gets a little less muddy after a rain than A, and is set back enough from the road to feel more private.

Potato Bottom C campsite is even further set back from the road, and is well-treed. It's also arguably the *least* muddy of the three after a rain — a statement which, while technically true, won't be of much comfort on a wet night.

# 8

## THE HARDSCRABBLE

Put yourself into 4WD-low here for the beginning of the climb up Hardscrabble at 65.7. The word "scrabble" has its roots in Middle Dutch, and encompasses concepts of barrenness, effort at the edges of one's ability, and a desperate groping around to find purchase. "Hardscrabble" is, to my thinking, one of the greatest names for a stretch of dirt road ever. The road through Hardscrabble is locally sometimes called the Walker Cut, for Mark Walker who is given credit for dynamiting the first widening of what was once a cattle trail around 1890. Walker also seems to have built the cabin at Fort Bottom.

65.8 A TIGHT TURN HERE, right below a pair of steel posts, requires most vehicles to back up and take a second pass at it. Hardscrabble, in general, is narrow and full of blind, tight turns.

66.2 STEEP SECTION HERE, with a lovely turnoff just after for anyone needing a break.

. . .

66.4 ONE OF my favorite pulloffs here with a great river view —
and a chance to inspect the 20° upslope just ahead. At the top
of that upslope is a large rock; if you're skinny enough, you can
avoid it, otherwise put one tire on it as you go over and carry on.

66.7 ANOTHER STEEP UPSLOPE HERE, with another flat spot on
top with views and room to pull off.

66.9 IT FEELS like the top here, with particularly striking views
down to the river; the road is still quite narrow.

67.2 TRAILHEAD for the Fort Bottom Trail, with a small area to
pull off the road. From near here you can see the road ahead
down by the river.

## Fort Bottom & the "Outlaw" Cabin

THE HIKE to the Fort Bottom Ruin is easily the most popular on
the White Rim Trail, in no small part because it's on *every* map.
There's a pull off with room for a few vehicles at the trailhead
(38.444222, -110.017500). The sign says it's about 1.5 miles
each way, and my GPS pretty much agreed; the first 0.6 miles is
downhill, the rest is uphill.

At the low point the trail becomes narrow and follows a
bit of a knife edge saddle that's getting narrower every year.
At some point the trail will probably have to be re-routed, as

this section is becoming harrowing, and erosion only works in one direction. But for now it's perfectly doable, if a bit unnerving.

*Walking back on the Fort Bottom Trail*

The "fort" is a round structure that's about 750 years old, constructed from rocks with timbers that suggest it was more than a single-story affair at one point. Theories about why it was built vary, but these days it's generally accepted to *not* have been a defensive structure. The scramble up to the small mesa top where the ruin sits is best accessed from the far side, and it takes a little searching to find the best way up. The reward is, of course, a close-up view of something of an ancient mystery, as well as a spectacular 360-degree view of the Green River and surrounding canyon.

From the "fort" looking to the north you'll see a small wood structure near the river, another 0.7 miles of hiking away. This is commonly called the Outlaw Cabin, although there's little evidence to suggest it was ever used as a hideout.

*Cabin on the Green River at Fort Bottom*

In 1895, the cabin was built as a sort of halfway house, meant to serve tuberculosis patients who would be traveling by river to a sanitarium that would be built near the confluence. Rancher Mark Walker is usually credited with the construction; he was a skilled carpenter by trade, who married into the Taylor family in 1884 and moved to Moab to be closer to his wife Augusta's parents.

The sanitarium never came to be, and the cabin likely saw most of its use from local cowboys and sheep herders looking to get out of the weather. In 2008 the structure of the cabin was reinforced and termite-proofed thanks to work and funding from the Vanishing Treasures Program, meaning it will hopefully be there to enjoy for years to come.

67.6 IF YOU look down to the left, the Hardscrabble campsites are visible — the small loop is Hardscrabble B Campsite.

68.0 A SMALL pull off here has another view of the Hardscrabble campsites, as well as the entire valley below.

68.1 THE DESCENT begins in earnest here, 15-20° downslopes that are sandy and rocky — hard scrabbly, if you will. There is much more sand on this side, and going in this (clockwise) direction on the trail makes for a far easier time.

*Switchbacks on Hardscrabble*

68.3 THIS STEP down into deep sand will test your approach

and departure angles, certainly — and make you glad you're not trying to get up it coming the other way. In fact, I'd suggest this obstacle is the single best argument for doing the White Rim Trail clockwise.

68.8 AFTER THIS DOWNSLOPE, you're definitely down; feel free to get out of 4WD-low.

68.9 A LEFT turn at this intersection leads to the Hardscrabble campsites. Hardscrabble A is 0.1 miles from the intersection; Hardscrabble B is 0.4 miles from the intersection. The access road here is definitely going to be muddy when wet.

---

## Hardscrabble Camps

*RIVER ACCESS and pleasant trees offer plenty of shade. Site B stays shady until mid-morning, and has a wide loop for turning around longer vehicles.*

IF THE MURPHY CAMPSITES were your reward for climbing up the Murphy Hogback, it might be argued the two campsites at Hardscrabble Camp are your reward for a successful trip over *their* namesake.

Again set quite close to the river, the Hardscrabble Campsites don't seem to suffer as greatly with mosquitoes; they do, however, suffer from muddy conditions when wet, although less at the camps themselves than over the spur road to access them. When dry, deep ruts — particularly on the way to Hardscrabble B — tell the story of how muddy the track will get after a good rain. Wider vehicles may feel a few branches scraping on either side as well.

Each of these sites has its own latrine, and few trees to speak of — at Hardscrabble A, there's a good-sized downed tree that provides an interesting backdrop, and perhaps half of what's needed to set up a hammock. One can pull around the loop that encircles the latrine here if need be, and it's a short push on foot through brush to reach the river.

Nearly a half-mile further down the spur road, Hardscrabble B's latrine inexplicably precedes the campsite itself by a good bit, but once you reach the camping boundaries you're in for a treat. There's a good-sized full pull-through turn-around down here, surrounded by some beautiful hoodoo rock formations. There are plenty of suitably-sized rocks for sitting, and a single decent shade tree. You're also close enough to the river to scramble down, and with a bit of luck you can find one of several small "beaches" on the other side of the tamarisk.

Both sites, as an added attraction, have a decent view up toward this side of the Hardscrabble road, and watching others negotiating the tight turns from the comfort of a camp chair is no small entertainment.

# 9

# UPHEAVAL CANYON TO MINERAL CANYON

P lan on being in 4WD-low for the short climb out from the Hardscrabble Camps spur. The upslope at 69.5 turns to the right at the top.

69.6 A NARROW STRETCH HERE, worth taking the time to ensure no one is coming the other way.

69.7 A 20° downslope here is just loose rocks on packed dirt, but the narrowness will certainly give wide vehicles pause.

69.8 DEEP RUTS through this section, again muddy when wet.

70.2 TRAILHEAD for the Upheaval Canyon Trail. Be in 4WD-low to cross down into the river bed here, and for the upslope on the other side. After a good rain, this river can be several inches deep; your target on the other side is straight across, hugging the inside of the left turn on the opposing bank. Keep your momentum up as you come to the other side, wet or dry it's quite sandy for the next 50-60 feet, followed by a rocky upslope.

----

## Upheaval Canyon Trail

BY ANY RECKONING it's certainly easier to walk *down* to a view of Upheaval Dome from the paved road up on the rim, but it's not too rough a hike *up* from the White Rim Trail if you've got the time — and you'll appreciate seeing things just that much more.

Upheaval Dome is a bit of an enigma. The massive depression behind Buck Mesa has always seemed out of place; for years, geologists thought perhaps it had formed from an enormous pocket of salt that had been exposed. A few had suggested a meteorite impact might have made the hole, mostly because it kind of looked like it — but it wasn't until recently that good evidence was unearthed to support that theory.

In fact, the impact theory is so compelling that unless someone pokes holes in the evidence, it's likely to stick. It's what I'm going with, at any rate.

Regardless of cause, it's a beautiful depression that's exposed a bounty of geological history. From the trailhead at the White Rim Trail, a 4-mile walk north (and uphill) will lead to the Syncline Loop Trail, which neatly circumnavigates the crater over a distance of just over 8 miles. If you have backpacking gear, consider breaking up that distance by reserving a backcountry campsite called "Syncline" up near the beginning of the loop trail (if you travel it *clockwise*, that is); it's available through the same online system used for White Rim Trail campsites.

· · ·

70.7 THE ISOLATED pinnacle on the Hardscrabble that you spotted from Potato Bottom is now, like the worst of the road, behind you.

70.9 THE JUNCTION with the Taylor Canyon Road. Taylor Canyon was named for a family of cattlemen who arrived in the 1890s led by patriarch Deb Taylor — generally believed to be the first to run stock in these canyons. Taylor Camp is 5.9 miles from here if you turn right.

----

## Taylor Camp

*THIS ONE-OF-A-KIND CAMPSITE IS ISOLATED, with no shade; the camping area has a fantastic view of nearby rock formations, although a third vehicle might find it cramped.*

OFTEN RELEGATED TO A SIDE TRIP, Taylor Camp is an inviting small site that's situated perfectly to view the Moses and Zeus rock formations (as well as their adjacent cousins). At the end of the day, that's really enough to make it worth a night's stay.

Taylor's usable footprint is relatively small; three vehicles here might feel a little crowded, and nothing provides shade, but it is utterly flat. There is a fair amount of traffic here, notably by climbers headed to the challenging pinnacles just ahead but also hikers coming down the Alcove Spring trail from above Upheaval Dome. I've sat with binoculars and watched climbers for hours here, and I'm still incredibly impressed how many top out this sheer tower in a given season; they're far enough away that in a still wind you can just hear a "whoop" of success when it happens.

But at the close of the day, here at the end of a spur that's more than twice as long as that leading to White Crack, the silence is complete, and engulfing. One could certainly stay at one of the Labyrinth sites and head up Taylor Canyon as an engaging day's drive, but there's nothing quite like watching the light fade around these formations.

*Taylor Camp*

The spur road continues past the campsite to a turnaround and trailhead, where a short hike puts one right among the giants. But even if you don't muster the energy for the walk, even right from the camping boundaries it's hard to take your eyes off the rocks, and I found an evening among them to be completely captivating.

## Taylor Canyon's "Monkey Rocks"

In 2011, Karl Tangren, one of the early stockmen who worked cattle right up until the park opened in the 1960s, delightedly told interviewer Jerry Shue how everyone knew about the "Monkey Rocks" where the old horse pathway heads up Trail Canyon.

---

"Well, if you ever seen a monkey just sittin' up you can't deny that...that sucker just as good as anybody could have chiseled, ya know."

---

And Ray Tibbets — son of old-time area cowboy Bill — told Shue he recalled the improvement to the road up Taylor Canyon had made it the best way to bring ore out of the mine in "Monkey Rock Canyon."

As late as 1974, the gorge was still being referred to as Monkey Rock Canyon by the National Park Service. But it's impossible to find the "Monkey Rocks" on any maps, at least by that name; the main formations are known as Moses and Zeus, and Monkey Rock Canyon is unlabeled.

So when did it change, and who renamed it?

Moses was already Moses, at least among tour companies and rock climbers, in October 1972 when Erin Bjornstad and Fred Beckey made a successful first ascent over three days. According to Bjornstad, Moab tour guide and rock shop owner Lin Ottinger told him Lin's mother named it Moses in the 1950's when she saw it for the first time (apparently breathlessly exclaiming "Holy Moses!"); in that spirit Bjornstad and Beckey named the smaller spire "Zeus" after anxiously watching lightning approach from the summit.

In case you're not sure which feature is which, Moses is the big one with a head, apparently looking to the right as seen from the campsite. Moses is sort of looking down at a rock called Thracian Mare, (named for one of the four man-eating horses tamed by Hercules, who fed them human flesh to do the job), first climbed by Ron Olevsky in 1983.

Zeus is the narrow spire just on the left. "Aphrodite" is the last on the left next to the rim, linked by a rocky saddle to Zeus (Aphrodite was first climbed in 1983 by Edward Webster and Chester Dreiman).

Of course, at this point you'll never unsee that monkey.

---

71.0 LABYRINTH CAMP sites A and B.

---

## Labyrinth Camps

*THESE ARE the last campsites before you exit the park, zero shade, zero trees, spectacular views.*

NAMED for the river canyon these sites overlook, a first impression of the Labyrinth Camps is that they're barren, rocky affairs, which is not untrue. The two sites feel small, but it's more that they are dwarfed by their environment. Shade comes only after sunset here, and there's little to block whatever wind might whip up or down the canyon. The two sites share a latrine, placed neatly between them.

Labyrinth A is situated up a hill, with few if any flat spots for cars, but plenty for tents. The site feels closer to the road than it is, probably because there's nothing but air and distance between you and it. Labyrinth B is much more level for vehicles, and is right above the river — a simply gorgeous spot by any measure, really, although it's an uphill hike to the latrine.

These are the last campsites before reaching the boundary of the national park, just 2.4 miles down the road. They are relatively close to the Upheaval Canyon Trailhead, and one could easily use these camps as a jumping-off point for either that trail or a day trip up Taylor Canyon.

---

71.2 A VERY NARROW stretch here right by the river, with some overhang that might make taller vehicles want a spotter; on the plus side, it's not as tight as it looks, and the river is beautiful — if a little close for comfort.

71.9 AT THIS POINT, the road improves considerably; rather than a dirt track, it's got the feel of a well-maintained county road.

72.3 A FEW RUTS HERE, again muddy when wet, break up an otherwise smooth surface. With less distraction on the road, don't forget to look at the spectacular cliffs that encircle you here; you're almost out of Canyonlands National Park.

72.8 MORE RUTS with tremendous mud potential.

. . .

73.2 AN INFORMATIONAL sign you see from the back here; the other side lets you know you're close to the border of the park.

73.3 ANOTHER SPEED BUMP HERE, healthy enough to discourage low-clearance vehicles coming the other way, I imagine.

73.4 THIS CATTLE guard marks the boundary, and you've officially left Canyonlands National Park.

75.1 A GOOD spot to again notice the canyon walls around you; it's perfectly beautiful, but just happens to not be inside the park.

76.7 A BOULDER halfway up the hill on the right does an incredible impression of one of the latrines from earlier campsites.

77.3 THE JUNCTION with the Horsethief Trail Road. A right turn here leads to the Mineral Bottom switchbacks, the pavement of Highway 313 in 12.9 miles, and Moab in 34 miles; a left turn over the hill leads on to the boat ramp, airfield, and Hell Roaring Canyon (see Chapter 10).

77.4 THE SWITCHBACKS up the Mineral Canyon Road begin. This road is best thought of as the Shafer Trail's wider, smoother cousin; generally, instead of rocky bumps, the worst of it here feels like light corrugation. In addition, low spots in the roadway — those most prone to being washed out in heavy rain — have been reinforced with concrete surfaces.

*Mineral Canyon Road*

78.1 Don't miss spotting a pair of wrecked vehicles off to the side here. They are older, and I'm not 100% convinced they weren't dumped there intentionally.

78.5 ONE OF a pair of upcoming pulloffs, both intentionally wide spots in the road where anyone pulling rafts or canoes on a trailer will appreciate the extra room. Views of the road from these are great, too, but try to leave room for long rigs headed to and from the boat ramp.

78.8 THE TOP of the switchbacks, with a good parking lot and interpretive sign. Nothing left from here but a long corrugated dirt road back to the highway.

81.0 SOME CELL phones will start working here, but it's a brief service spot that ends in 4 miles.

89.7 ANOTHER AREA of spotty cell service that lasts less than a half mile.

92.0 HIGHWAY 313, and a return to paved roads. A right turn will take you to the Island in the Sky Visitor Center in 10 miles; a left turn here will take you back to Highway 191. Once on Highway 191, a right turn and about 11 more miles will put you in Moab.

# 10

# HELL ROARING CANYON

W hile a drive to Hell Roaring Canyon isn't on the White Rim Trail, it's incredibly close and historically significant, so I'm including it as a side trip — and I highly recommend taking it. Mileage here is measured from the beginning of the White Rim Trail at the Shafer Trail sign (mile 0.0), and picks up right from mile 77.3, the junction at Mineral Bottom Road — where you'll turn left instead of right for this side trip.

78.3 THE MINERAL Bottom Boat Ramp and its *great* latrines; the area is day use only, no camping.

78.7 TO YOUR right here is the road up Mineral Canyon, worth exploring if you've got plenty of time.

78.8 THE ROAD that goes off to the left here leads to a surprisingly popular backcountry airstrip; keep the roadway clear, particularly if there are planes on the ground nearby.

79.0 THE WINDSOCK for the airport can (usually) be seen on the left; the road to here is usually quite smooth.

80.2 A TURNAROUND HERE, with a sign noting a "dead end" ahead. While this is technically true, the road doesn't truly end for a few miles. However, if you've got no stomach for the narrow, rough, branch-enshrouded road from here to Hell Roaring Canyon, this is the spot to stop. On a dry day, the road won't challenge a skinny vehicle any more than the worst of the White Rim Trail; however you can expect branches (and perhaps rocks) to scratch down the side of even a narrow vehicle, and the drop to the river is *right* on the edge of your tires. Wider truck owners, feel free to walk from here; it's only about 1.6 miles.

80.8 THE SQUEEZE here is particularly narrow, followed by a usually-left-open gate. The general rule is to leave gates as you find them, open or closed; use your judgment here.

80.9 A DIP through a small wash here is loose and rocky; if you're not already in 4WD-low, you should be.

81.0 A BOULDER here makes a narrow road *really* narrow.

.   .   .

81.2 THIS ROCKY mess is short-lived, but bumpy.

81.8 IF YOU squeezed by the last turn down, you've arrived at Hell Roaring Canyon. The road does continue up the canyon from here, but becomes increasingly difficult until it peters out completely. On the right is the sign marking the Denis Julien inscription.

*Sandstone block at Hell Roaring Canyon*

## Denis Julien (and other vandals)

IF THE YEAR 1836 seems like a really long time ago, it's because it was — more than 180 years ago at the time of this writing. For some context, at the beginning of 1836, Betsy Ross was still alive, the Civil War was still 25 years in the future, and Teddy Roosevelt wouldn't even be *born* for another two decades.

Denis Julien's inscription on a boulder in what would be named Hell Roaring Canyon even predates John Wesley Powell's exploration of the Green and Colorado Rivers by more than thirty years — which means, of course, when Julien passed through, the canyon wasn't "Hell Roaring" yet.

*Dirt track up Hell Roaring Canyon*

A successful fur trader and trapper, Julien was almost in his 60s by the time he entered Utah's canyon country in search of beaver and otter — and he left his name in a handful of places up and down the rivers during a period spanning more than 10 years. The 1836 carving is the only one in Canyonlands National Park, although there is one at Arches that may or may not be authentic.

One of the fascinating things about this carving is the depiction of a boat with a mast — implying that, as his other inscriptions would suggest, he sailed upriver, using the common upstream winds. It's likely he would have been the first to accomplish a "round trip" journey on the Green River.

Hidden among the more contemporary ill-conceived graffiti cluttering the sandstone are a handful of other historically interesting names. The two Wolvertons were a father-son gold prospecting team who passed through in 1905. Worthy, McFarland, and Adams all worked for the U.S. Reclamation Service (which later became the Bureau of Reclamation) and likely camped here during a 1914 expedition.

The site is listed on the National Register of Historic Places; defacing or damaging the inscriptions isn't just inconsiderate, it's against federal law. The Bureau of Land Management has placed a register box near the site for those so inclined to share their name and thoughts — rather than doing it on the sandstone wall.

# INDEX

# BIBLIOGRAPHY & SUGGESTED
# READING

Bjørnstad, Eric. *Desert Rock: A Climber's Guide to the Canyon Country of the American Southwest Desert*. Colorado: Chockstone Press, 1988.

Castleton, Kenneth B. *Petroglyphs and Pictographs of Utah, Vol. I & II*. Utah: Utah Museum of Natural History, 1987.

Chenoweth, William L. *Uranium Deposits of the Canyonlands Area*. Colorado: U.S. Energy Research and Development Administration, 1975.

Crampton, C. Gregory. *Standing Up Country*. Arizona: Rio Nuevo Publishers, 1964.

Day, David. *Canyonlands National Park: Favorite Jeep Roads & Hiking Trails*. Utah: Rincon Publishing Co., 2004

Dean, H. Clay. *Desert Bighorn Sheep in Canyonlands National Park*. Utah: Utah State University, 1977.

deVergie, Paul C. and Carlson, William A. *Investigation of the "C" Group Area, San Juan County, Utah.* Tennessee: U.S. Atomic Energy Commission, Technical Information Service, 1953.

*Draft Environmental Statement, Proposed Wilderness, Canyonlands National Park, Utah.* Colorado: National Park Service Denver Service Center, 1974.

Johnson, David W. *Canyonlands: The Story Behind the Scenery.* Nevada: K.C. Publications, Inc., 1989.

Kelsey, Michael R. *Hiking, Biking, and Exploring Canyonlands National Park and Vicinity.* Utah: Kelsey Publishing, 2013.

Knipmeyer, Jim. *The Howland & Wheeler 1894 Inscription(s).* Utah: Journal of Colorado Plateau River Guides, 2003.

Lathrop, Marguerite. *Don't Fence Me In.* Colorado: Johnson Publishing Co., 1972.

Lavender, David. *Colorado River Country.* New York: E.P. Dutton, Inc., 1982.

Lavender, David. *One Man's West.* New York: Doubleday & Company, 1964.

Lohman, S. W. *The Geologic Story of Canyonlands National Park.* Colorado: U.S. Geological Survey, 1974.

McClenahan, Owen. *Utah's Scenic San Rafael.* Utah: Owen McClenahan, 1986.

Mehls, Steven F. *Canyonlands National Park, Arches National Park, and*

*Natural Bridges National Monument Historic Resource Study.* Colorado: National Park Service Rocky Mountain Regional Office, 1986.

Murphy, Miriam B. *A History of Wayne County.* Utah: Utah State Historical Society, 1999.

Osborn, Alan J. et al. *Aboriginal Lithic Raw Material Procurement in Glen Canyon and Canyonlands, Southeastern Utah.* Nebraska: Midwest Archeological Center, National Park Service, 1993.

Powell, Allan Kent. *San Juan County, Utah: People, Resources, and History.* Utah: Utah State Historical Society, 1983.

Rigby, J. Keith. *Northern Colorado Plateau.* Iowa: Kendall/Hunt Publishing Company, 1976.

Schmieding, Samuel J. *From Controversy to Compromise to Cooperation: the Administrative History of Canyonlands National Park.* National Park Service, 2008.

Sheire, James. *Historic Resource Study: Cattle Raising in the Canyons.* Colorado: National Park Service Denver Service Center, 1972.

Tipps, Betsy L., La Fond, André D., and Birnie, Robert I. *Cultural Resource Investigations near White Crack, Island-in-the-Sky District, Canyonlands National Park, Utah.* Colorado: National Park Service Intermountain Regional Office, 1996.

Williams, David B. and Fagan, Damian. *A Naturalist's Guide to the White Rim Trail.* Washington: Wingate Ink, 2007.

Zoellner, Tom. *Uranium: War, Energy, and the Rock that Shaped the World.* New York: Penguin Books, 2009

# ABOUT THE AUTHOR

Robb Magley's career in outdoor writing began in the 1990s covering lesser-known destinations for fledgling adventure magazines; in the years since he has earned seven journalism awards from the Colorado Press Association for work at two newspapers, has been a featured author on Colorado Public Radio, and installed a bathtub by himself. Despite still taking notes with a pencil like some Neanderthal, "The White Rim Trail: Mile by Mile" is his second book about a Four-Corners-area National Park.

Made in the USA
Columbia, SC
17 February 2019